THE GENEALOGIST'S GUIDE

LATIN TO ENGLISH TERMINOLOGY & ABBREVIATIONS

GENEALOGIST'S GUIDES
BOOK 1

INTERNATIONAL INSTITUTE OF GENEALOGICAL STUDIES

Please direct inquiries regarding orders, copyright, or other matters to:

INTERNATIONAL INSTITUTE OF GENEALOGICAL STUDIES

Telephone: 1-800-580-0165 Ext. 1 (in North America)

Email: **info@genealogicalstudies.com**

The Genealogist's Guide: Latin to English Terminology & Abbreviations

Printed in Missoula, Montana, by GS Books,

1st Edition: June 2025

Paperback ISBN: 978-1-957132-13-6

Ebook ISBN: 978-1-957132-10-5

PDF ISBN: 978-1-957132-11-2

TABLE OF CONTENTS

ABOUT THE GENEALOGIST'S GUIDE...

"No more scary Latin roadblocks!"

The Genealogist's Guide: Latin to English Terminology and Abbreviations unlocks centuries of family history trapped in Latin records across the world. This essential reference guide translates the most common Latin terms, phrases, and abbreviations found in church registers, civil documents, and genealogical records from medieval times through the 19th century.

Whether you're deciphering baptismal records, marriage certificates, or burial entries, this comprehensive glossary provides instant access to accurate English translations. Organized alphabetically, it's the indispensable tool every family historian needs to bridge the language gap and discover ancestral stories.

Brought to you by the International Institute of Genealogical Studies, this genealogist's companion tool includes space to add terms and abbreviations you run across, note pages, and is available in PDF, eBook, and paperback. Small enough to carry everywhere! Handy help for modern documents and contracts as well. Stop letting Latin be a barrier to your research-start reading your ancestors' records today.

INTRODUCTION

Genealogists encounter the Latin language in various historical documents and time periods. Latin is common in religious records, but also in estate, courts, land records, and more. This publication was created to assist in your research when transcribing and translating Latin within historical through modern documents.

Latin is touched on in many of the International Institute of Genealogical Studies' courses and discussed in more detail in the *Latin for Genealogists* course through the International Institute of Genealogical Studies. This publication has been compiled from those courses and other publications to help in your research success.

Only Latin to English translations for words and phrases have been provided, as well as male and female names. The abbreviation list provides the term in Latin as well as English.

In some instances, after the term or phrase is defined, the type of record the Latin word may be found in is indicated in parentheses (e.g., Probate, Quitclaim, Lease, etc.)

Each section has additional space to add terms as you discover them. Remember, not all letters in various alphabets exist in the Latin alphabet.

The International Institute of Genealogical Studies invites you to use this book as part of your everyday genealogical experience and your reference library.

Susanna de Groot, PLCGS, deserves a lot of praise for her diligence in compiling this work from our many courses and support materials written by so many individuals over the years. Thank you to our IIGS staff for all they do daily to serve our students and provide excellent online education opportunities via GenealogicalStudies.com and GenealogySocial.com.

With appreciation to all who have shared considerable knowledge allowing growth in the genealogy industry!

If you'd like to learn more about a genealogical education, please visit us at GenealogicalStudies.com. We look forward to serving your educational goals and supporting your continuing research.

Angela Breidenbach, PLCGS

Executive Director,
International Institute of Genealogical Studies
& GenealogySocial.com, social media exclusively for genealogists and family historians.

WEBSITES

The following is a list of websites to aid in deciphering the Latin language found in genealogical research documents.

FamilySearch - Research Wiki - Latin Genealogical Word List

https://www.familysearch.org/en/wiki/Latin_Ge nealogical_Word_List

Internet Archive - Parish Register Latin: An Introduction

https://archive.org/details/parishregister la00crus/page/n5

Internet Archive - The Record Interpreter: A collection of abbreviations, Latin words and names used in English historical manuscripts and records

https://archive.org/details/recordinterprete00 martiala/page/n3/mode/2up

Latin Dictionary

https://www.online-latin-dictionary.com/

The Latin Library

http://thelatinlibrary.com/

ThoughtCo - Humanities - History & Culture - Latin
Genealogical Terms

**https://www.thoughtco.com/latin-genealogical-
word-list-1422735**

Yandex Translate - Latin-English online translator and
dictionary

**https://translate.yandex.com/translator/Latin-
English**

LATIN WORDS AND PHRASES
DEFINED - A

a mensa et thoro ● "from table and bed", a legal separation

a quo ● from whom

ab ● from

ab infinitum ● endlessly, for ever

ab initio ● from the beginning

ab intestato ● intestate

abavia ● great-great-grandmother

abavus ● great-great-grandfather

abdormitus ● died

abdormivit ● he/she died

abiit ● he/she died

abjuro ● to deny under oath

ablutus est ● he was baptised

abortivus ● prematurely born

abscessus • death

abstersus • baptised

acatholicus • Protestant, non-catholic

acquietus est • he/she died

actio • action, suit

actuarius • notary, clerk

ad • to

ad diem • to the appointed day

ad quod damnum • to what damage

ad quod hoc presens scriptum pervenit • to whom this present writing comes ... (Quitclaim)

ad summan • to conclude

adnotatio • remark

advocatus • lawyer

adulterium • adultery

aeger • sick

ædituus • verger

æquus • equal

æt • at the age of

ætas • age

ætate minoris • of a younger age, underage

ætati • age

affirmanti non neganti incumbit probatio ● burden of proof is on him who affirms, not on him who denies

age dies vitae ● days of life

agillarius ● [occupation] hayward

agnatus ● blood relative from the paternal line

agnus ● lamb

Agnus Dei ● the Lamb of God (Jesus Christ)

agricola ● husbandman, farmer

ainescia ● legal right of eldest child

alba firma ● rent paid in silver, white rents or quit rents payable in silver [black rents were paid in work or goods]

alia enormia ● other wrongdoings

alias ● known by another name

alias dictus ● otherwise known as, [given] a false name

alimosina ● alimony, compassion

aloverium ● purse

alumnus ● pupil

amicus ● friend

amita ● father's sister, aunt

amita magna ● father's aunt

amita maior ● father's great-aunt

amita maxima ● father's great-great-aunt

ancilla ● female servant

ancipitus usus ● of questionable use

angelus ● angel

Anglia ● England

anima ● soul, spirit

animus deserendi ● intention of deserting, e.g. a spouse

animus furandi ● intention of stealing

animus revocandi ● intention of revoking

anno domino ● in the year of the Lord

anno Regni ● year of the reign

anno urbis conditae ● the year of the founded city

annuatim ● annually

annus ● year

annus bissextus ● leap year

ante cibum ● before meals

ante meridiem ● before noon

antedictus ● aforesaid

antenatio ● legal right of eldest child

antiqua statua ● statutes passed before reign of Edward III

antiquus ● senior, old

anus ● old woman

aperire ● to open, to uncover

apothecarius ● shopkeeper

aprilis ● April

4

arbiter • witness

arbitium • judgement

Archidiaconus • Archdeacon

Archiepiscopus • Archbishop

arcularius • carpenter, cabinet maker

argentarius • banker

armiger • gentleman, squire, knight

arrento • rent

arreragium • arrears

articuli super chartas • the law of 1300 confirming Magna Carta

assero • assert, claim

assisa vertitur in juratam • the original writ began with the assize, later required a jury

assurantia • conveyance

assuro • swear, convey [land]

atavia • great-great-great-grandmother

atavus • great-great-great-grandfather

attornasse et in loco meo possuisse • letters of attorney; to have acted as attorney and have acted in my place have ...

augustus • August

aurifaber • goldsmith

auriga • cart driver

auster • south

aut • or

avia • grandmother

avunculus • mother's brother, uncle

avunculus magnus • mother's uncle

avunculus maior • mother's great-uncle

avunculus maximus • mother's great-great-uncle

avus • grandfather

2

LATIN WORDS AND PHRASES DEFINED - B

bacallarius ● bachelor

baillivus ● bailiff

ballistrarius ● gunsmith

bannis ● banns

bannorum liber ● marriage banns register

bannum ● bann, marriage announcement

baptisatus ● christened, baptised

baptisma ● christening, baptism

baptismus ● christening, baptism

baptizandi ● baptised

baptizatorum liber ● baptismal register

baronettus ● baronet

baronis ● baron

bastardus ● bastard

beatus • blessed

benedictio • blessing

beneficium inventarii • inventory benefit

bercarius • shepherd

bibiopega • bookbinder

biduum • two-year period

bonus • good, kind

burriarius • dairyman

3

LATIN WORDS AND PHRASES DEFINED - C

cadaver ● corpse

caelibis ● single, unmarried

cælebs ● unmarried, bachelor, widower

cæteris paribus ● things being equal

Caledonia ● Scotland

caligarius ● boot-maker

calumnio ● claim

Cambria ● Wales

canonicus ● cannon

capella ● chapel

Capellanus ● Chaplain

capitagium ● poll tax

capt et jurat ● sworn

Caput Jejunii ● Ash Wednesday

Caramentranum ● Shrove Tuesday

carbonarius ● collier

carnifex ● butcher, murderer

carpentarius ● carpenter

carta ● deed

carus ● loved

cas ● house, cottage

casale ● estate

catallum ● chattle, moveable goods

cataster ● land

Catholicus ● Catholic

caupo ● innkeeper, tavern owner

causa mortis ● because of death

causation ● plea

causidicus ● lawyer, attorney

caveat ● let him beware. In an estate file, "a search for caveat" is a search of court records to ensure a petition for probate or letters of administration hadn't previously been filed, or other legal proceeding hadn't commenced which would interfere with the probate / administration process.

centesimus ● one hundredth

centum ● one hundred

certiorari ● to be informed of. A written order issued by a higher court to a lower court to produce a certified record of a particular case.

certus ● certain, sure

chevagium ● poll tax

cibus ● food

cimeterium ● cemetery

cippus ● gravestone

circa ● around, approximate

circulus ● region

civis ● citizen

clausit ● he finished, concluded, died

Clausum Pentecostes ● Trinity Sunday

clericus ● clerk, clergyman

clericu sparochialis ● parish clerk

cleronomus ● heir

coelebs ● bachelor

coemeterium ● cemetery

cognatio ● known

cognomen ● surname

cohæredes sunt quasi unum corpus ● co-heirs are considered as one person

colonus ● settler, farmer, peasant

Comes ● Count

comitatus ● county

Comitissa ● Countess

commater • godmother

commuratis • fornication

compater • godfather

concedo • grant, pardon

cond testamentum • make a will

confirmatio • confirmation

confirmavit • confirmed

conjuncti sunt • they were joined [in marriage]

conjux • wife

concepta est • she was pregnant

conditio • condition

conjugatus • married

conjuncti sunt • they were joined in marriage

conjux • spouce

consobrina • female cousin

consobrinus • male cousin on maternal side

consul • magistrate

contra • against

contractio • [marriage] contract

contradico plegium • refuse

contradicito • objection

coopertor • roofer, thatcher

cophinarius • basketmaker

copulation • marriage

copulati • couple

copulati sunt • joined in marriage

copulationis • of marriage

copulatus • married

coram • before, in the presence of

coram judice • before a judge

corarius • currier, Tanner

coupiator • woodman

corpus • body

creta • chalk

crysomme • child of an unchurched mother, or a mother not cleansed after giving birth

cui in vita • action allowing a widow to recover her lands, alienated by the coverture of her husband

cujus • whose

cultellarius • cutler

cultororis • farmer, husbandman

cum • with

cum cibo • with food

cum dispensatione in bannis • with dispensation by banns

cum testamento annexo • with will annexed or attached

cuprifaber • coppersmith

curator • guardian

curia • court

curia advisari vult • the court wishes to be advised [judgement delayed]

Curia Baroni • Court Baron (Manorial Court)

Curia Regis • King's Court

custodia • custody

custos • custodian

custumarias • customary tenant

cyrographum • handwritten [A document in duplicate or multiplicate on a single sheet with "cyrographum" written across the middle.]

LATIN WORDS AND PHRASES
DEFINED - D

damnum • damage, injury

dare ad remanentiam • to grant a reversionary right

dare de fine • to pay a fine

dare in manu • to make a pledge

dare intellegi • to understand

data apud ... predicto in die Iovis post octavas • Dated at ..., Thursday after the Octave

datus • date

de bonis grant • Administration taken over by another administrator after death of first one.

de bonis non administratis • of goods unadministered by. Second administrator who took over after first one died.

de die in diem • from day to day

de ingressu • a writ of entry

de jure • by right

de recte • a writ of right

de son tort demesne • of his own wrong

de ventre inspiciendo • If a widow claims to be with child, an heir could produce this writ to examine whether she was with child or not, and to keep her under surveillance until delivery.

debitor • debtor

debitum • debt

debitum principal • total debt

Decanatus • Deanery

Decanus • Deacon

decem • ten

decembri • December

decessit • he died

decessit sine martis • died with mother alive

decessit sine partis • died with father alive

decessit sine prole • died without issue surviving

decessit sine prole femina • died without female issue

decessit sine prole legitima • died without legitimate issue

decessit sine prole mascula • died without male issue

decessit sine prole superstes • died without surviving issue

decessit vita matris • died in mother's lifetime

decessit vita patris • died in father's lifetime

decessus • death

decima • tithe

decimus • tenth

decretum • decree

dedi, concessi et hac presenta carta confirmavi • have given, granted and by this my present charter confirmed.

defalta • default

defensor • defender

deflorata • not virginal

defuit • died

defuncta • dead

defunctorum liber • death register

defunctus • dead, deceased

defunctus est • he died

Dei • God

denarius • penny

denatus • dead

denatus est • he died

derelictus • abandonded

desponsatus • engaged

dexter • right [direction]

didymus • twin

die mensis • day of month

dies • day

dies Adoratus • Good Friday

dies Cinerum • Ash Wednesday

dies Dominicus • Sunday

dies Felicissimus • Easter Day

dies Iovis • Thursday

dies Iovis Absolutionis • Maundy Thursday

dies Lune • Monday

dies Magnus • Easter Day

dies Mandati • Maundy Thursday

dies Martis • Tuesday

dies Mercurii • Wednesday

dies non juridicus • day on which no legal business can be transacted, e.g. Christmas, Easter

dies Palmarum • Palm Sunday

dies Paschalis • Easter Sunday

dies Sabbatinus • Sabbath Day

dies Saturni • Saturday

dies Veneris • Friday

dies Veneris Sanctus • Good Friday

dieta • one day's work

dilectos in Christo • beloved in Christ

Diocesis • Diocese

discessit • he died

discipulus • pupil, disciple

dispensatis • dispensed

doageria • dowager [a widow who holds property or title]

doli capax • capable of crime

doli incapax • incapable of crime, e.g. a minor

doliarius • cooper

dolus • fraud

domanicum • householder

domesticus • servant

domicellus • young nobleman, servant

domicilium • residence

domina • wife, mistress of home

Dominica • Sunday

dominus • lord, landlord

domus • home, house

domus sua cuique est tutissimum refugium • every man's house is his refuge

dona clandestine sunt semper suspiciosa • clandestine gifts are always suspicious

donatio • donation, gift

donatio inter vivos • a gift between the living

donatio nortis cauda • a gift in anticipation of a person's death

donatio mortis causa • donation due to death

donatio propter nuptias • a settlement made by the husband to his wife

donum • gift

dos • dowry

dos perfectiva • father's dowry

duarium • dowry

dum casta vixerit • while she continues to live a chaste life

dum fuit non compos mentis • while he was not of sound mind

dum sola • while single, not married

duo • two

duodecim • twelve

duodecimus • twelfth

duodevicesimus • eighteenth

duodeviginti • eighteen

durante absentia • while absent

durante minore ætate • during the age of minority

durante viduitate • during widowhood

durante vita • during life

Dux • Duke, leader

5

LATIN WORDS AND PHRASES
DEFINED - E

eat inde sine die • he can go without a day, he is dismissed from the suit

ecclesia • church

edificator • architect, builder

ego • I

elemosina • alms

emenda • fine

emendo • pay a fine

eodem • same, ditto

eodem anno • same year

eodem die • same day

eodem mense • same month

Epiphanie domini • Ephipany of the Lord

Episcopus • Bishop

et • and

et alii • and others

et cetera • and so forth

et ego vero predictus • And I, truly the said ...

et nos • we

et pro hac donacion • and for this gift

et uxor • and wife

ex contractu • arising out of contract

ex curia • out of court

ex delicto • arising out of wrong doings

ex maleficio non oritur contractus • a contract cannot arise out of an illegal act

ex mero motu • one's own free will

ex officio • arising out of one's office

ex officio promoto • promoted from office

ex parte altera testatur quod • of the other part witnesses that ... (Lease)

ex partie una et ... • of the one part ...

executor • administrator

executrix • female administrator

exempli gratia • for example

exemplo • copy document

exhalavit animam • he exhaled his soul, died

exonero ● discharge

expensum ● payment

extracta ● estreat, copy for court

extremum munitus ● last rites given

6

LATIN WORDS AND PHRASES
DEFINED - F

faber • smith, blacksmith, craftsman

faber argentarius • silversmith

faber aurantarius • goldsmith

faber ferrarius • blacksmith

faber lignarius • carpenter

faber rotarius • wheelwright

facere homagium • pay homage

factum proband • facts which need proof

familia • family

fateor • confess

februarius • February

fecunda • pregnant, fertilized

femina • woman

feodarius • tenant

feodotalis • fealty, service

feria • day of the week, fair, holiday

Feria prima • Lord's Day

Feria Quarta • Wednesday

Feria Quinta • Thursday

Feria Secunda • Monday

Feria Septima • Saturday

Feria Sexta • Friday

Feria Tertia • Tuesday

feriae • a holiday

festivitas • festival, gaiety

festum • feast

Festum Christi • Christmas

Festum Olivarum • Palm Sunday

Festum Omnium Sanctorum • All Saint's Day

Festum Palmarum • Palm Sunday

fiat • make

fiat capsula • make a capsule

fiat justitia • let justice be done

fiat unguentum • make an ointment

figulus • potter

filia • daughter

filia legitimus • a legitimate daughter of

26

filia populae ● illegitimate daughter

filiam ● aughter

filium ● son

filius ● son

filius legitimus ● a legitimate son of

filius nullius ● nobody's son, a bastard

filius populi ● illegitimate son

finis finem litibus imponi ● a fine terminates legal proceedings

firmiter teneri et obligari ● am firmly bound and obligated (Bond)

focagium ● hearth tax

focus ● hearth

folio ● page

forestarius ● forester

forma capellæ ● Chancery form

fortis ● strong

fortis mistura ● strong mixture

franchilanus ● freeman

franciplegius ● free pledge

frater ● brother

fratris filia ● brother's daughter, niece

fratris filius ● brother's son, nephew

fraus ● fraud

fuagium • hearth tax

fuit • was

functus officio • having discharged his duty

fundus cum instrumento • a farm including the necessary stock and implements

fundus instructus • a farm with furnishings, stock, and implements

funerius • ropemaker

furnarius • baker

7

LATIN WORDS AND PHRASES
DEFINED - G

gablum • rent

Gardianus • Churchwarden

gardinarius • gardener

gemellae • twins — females

gemelli • twins — males or male and female

gemini • twins

geminus • a twin

gener • son-in-law

genitores • parents

genitus est • he was born

gersuma • fine

gersumo • pay a fine

gigno • beget, produce

gilda mercatoria • guild merchant who can levy payments on foreign traders

glos • [husband's] sister-in-law

grassator • robber

gravida • pregnant

grocerus • grocer

gubernium • domain

8

LATIN WORDS AND PHRASES DEFINED - H

habeas corpus • a requirement to produce the body

habendum et tenendum omnnia predicta terras • to have and to hold all the said lands (Deed of gift)

habere • to have, to hold

habere facias seisinam • A writ allowing a person to have feudal possession of a freehold estate which is recovered in an action.

habitatio • home, residence

hec conventio facta inter • this agreement made between ... (Agreement)

hec est finalis concordia • this is the final agreement (Fine)

hec indentura facta inter ... • this indenture made between ... (Lease)

haec • this

heredes • heirs

hereditamentum • hereditament

hereditatio • inheritance

heres • heirs

Hibernia • Ireland

hiis testibus • there being witnesses

hodie • today

homagium • homage

hora • hour

hora somni • at bedtime

horarius • clockmaker

hortarius • gardener

hostellarius • innkeeper

humationis • burial

humatus est • he was buried

humoare • to bury

hydragyrum • Mercury

9

LATIN WORDS AND PHRASES
DEFINED - I

ianuarius • January

ibi • there, in that place

ibidem • same place, book, date, etc.

id est • that is

ideo • therefore

ignorantia juris quod quisque scire tenetur non excusant • ignorance of the law which everyone should know is not excusable

ignoti • illegitimate

ignotes parentibus • unknown parents

ignoti parentis • of unknown parentage

ignotis • unknown

illegitima • illegitimate

illegitimus • illegitimate

impediens • defendant

implacita • to plead

impotens ignotus • feebleminded

impregnata • pregnant

imprimis • Firstly, first of all, especially

in Anglia non est interregnum • In England, the King never dies, as his heir is proclaimed upon death.

in articulo mortis • at the point of death

in bonis • in the goods of

in commendam • in trust

in curia • in open court

in cuius rei testimonium huic presenti carte sigillum meum apposui • in witness of which thing I have affixed my seal to this present charter

in die nomine Amen • in the name of God Amen

in forma pauperis • in the character of a pauper

in futuro • in future

in loco parentis • in place of a parent

in misericordia • in mercy

in nomini • in the name of

in pais • in the country of

in partibus transmarinis • foreign parts, i.e., outside England, Ireland, Scotland, and Wales

in perpetuu • for ever

in pleno • in full

in pura viduetate ● in pure widowhood [married women couldn't dispose of property]

in pura virginitate ● in pure virginhood [spinster]

in situ ● in its original place

in statu quo ● in the former position

in terrorum ● [clause] A stipulation in a will that has to be complied with or the legatee forfeits the inheritance. (Probate)

in totidem verbis ● in so many words

incerti cognominis ● uncertain family name

inculpamentum ● accusation

indebite ● dues

indentura ● indenture

indulgeo ● grant an indulgence

infans ● a child under the age of seven

infanti proximus ● a child under the age of seven, who can speak without understanding

infantia ● childhood

ingenus ● yeoman, freeman

inhumatus ● not buried

initiatus est ● he was baptised

injuria ● a legal wrong

inops consilii ● without advice

inquisitio ● inquiry

inscripsit ● has inscribed

insulta • assault

intempo • to accuse

inter cibos • between meals

inter vivos • between the living

interesse termini • one term's interest at the start of a lease

intestatus • intestate

instante • immediate, at the present moment

intramuscular • into the muscle

introitus • entry

inupta • unmarried

inventarium • inventory

ipse • self

ipsissima verba • identical words

ipso facto • by the fact

Isti Sunt Dies • Passion Sunday

iter • journey

iunius • June

iulius • July

iuncti sunt • they were joined, married

iure ux(oris) • inherited by the right of his wife

10

LATIN WORDS AND PHRASES
DEFINED - J

judex • judge

judicia publica • public prosecution

judicium • judgement, court

junius • June

julius • July

juncti sunt • they were joined, married

jura regalia • sovereign rights

juramentus exhibitum fuit • sworn certificate was produced

jurator • juror

juratores sunt judices facti • juries judge facts

juratus • sworn

juravit • he swore, oath

juris • law

jurisconsultus • jurist, lawyer

jurista • lawyer

juro • swear

jus • law

jus canonicum • Canon Law, the law of the church

jus civile • Common Law

jus mariti • husband's rights

jus non scriptum • unwritten law which arises from use

jus privatum • law between private parties

jus publicum privatorum pactis mutari non potest • private agreements cannot supersede public law

Jus sanguinis • regardless of where a child is born, the child's nationality is dependent on parental nationalities

Jus soli • (or right of the soil) any baby born on a country's soil, regardless of nationality or birth country of the parents, acquires citizenship at birth

Justiciarius • Judge

justifico • justify

LATIN WORDS AND PHRASES
DEFINED - K

Currently there are no "K" words or phrases. Use this space to write words and phrases you discover in your genealogical research journey.

LATIN WORDS AND PHRASES
DEFINED - L

laborarius • labourer

lanarius • wool merchant

lanius • butcher

lapidariu • stonemason

laudare • to praise

lautus est • he was baptised

lavatus est • he was baptised

lavo • I baptise, wash

legalis monetæ Angliæ • legal money of England

legatum nominis • a legacy of debt

legitimatus per rescriptum principis • legitimate by subsequent marriage

legrewita • fine for adultery

lettere patentes • letters patent

levantes ● godparents

levir ● [husband's] brother-in-law

Levita ● Deacon

lex ● statute, law

lex domicilii ● the law of the place of a person's residence

lex non scripta ● unwritten law or Common Law

lex scripta ● Statute Law

liber ● book, volume

liberi ● children

libertinus ● freedman

liberum tenementum ● freehold land or property

libro ● book, volume

ligati sunt ● they were married

lignarius ● cabinet-maker, carpenter

limitat ● Limited Grant of Administration (Probate)

littera ● letter

lo ● an exclamation to express joy or pain, akin to "Oh" in English

loco ● to lease, place

locus ● place

locus sigilli ● the place of the seal [after a signature on a will]

loquela ● [law] suit

13

LATIN WORDS AND PHRASES
DEFINED - M

magister ● teacher, master

magna aetas ● great age

magnum oppidum ● large town

magnus ● large, great

magnus rex ● great king

maius ● May

malus ● bad, evil

mane ● morning

manerium ● manor

manser ● bastard

manus ● hand

mare ● sea

martia ● wife

mariti ● married couple

marito • marry

maritus • husband

martius • March

masculus • male

mater • mother

matertera • aunt on maternal side

matertera magna • mother's aunt

matertera maior • mother's great-aunt

matertera maxima • mother's great-great-aunt

matrimonium • marriage

matrimonium sacrament • of Holy Matrimony or marriage

matrina • godmother

matrina fuit • godmother was

matriomonio conjunctio fuere • they were joined in marriage

medicus • doctor

memorandum quod • remember that [phrase used at start of nuncupative will]

mensis • month

mercator • merchant

meridianus • noon

meus • my, mine

miles • soldier

mille • one thousand

millesimus • one thousandth

molitor • builder, miller

mistura • mixture

morbus • sickness, disease

More Novo • New Style (Calendar) [Gregorian calendar]

More Vetere • Old Style (Calendar) [Julian calendar]

mors • death

mortis • death

mortua • dead

mortuarium • duty paid on death of tenant

mortuus • dead, deceased

mortuus est • he died

mulier • woman, wife

multus • many

mundus • world

murarius • mason

mutatis mutandis • the required changes being made

14

LATIN WORDS AND PHRASES DEFINED - N

Natalis Dies • Christmas, Birth Day

nativitas • birth

naturales liberi • natural children, not necessarily born in wedlock

naturalis • illegitimate

natus • born, birth

natus est • he was born

nauta • sailor

nemo debet bis puniri pro uno delicto • no one should be punished twice for the same fault

nemo est hæres viventis • no one is the heir of a living person

nemo tenetur se ipsum accusare • no one is required to incriminate himself

neosponsus • male newlywed

nepos • grandson

nepis • granddaughter

nisi • a decree or order, to take effect unless a person involved gives evidence why it shouldn't; the order becomes absolute

nobis • us

nocte • night

nomen • first name

nomen baptisati • name of baptised

nomen sacerdotis • name of the assistant priest

nomina baptisatorum • name of the baptised

nomina defunctorum • name of the dead

nomina nuptorum • name of the married

nomina parentum • names of parents

nomina sepultorum • name of the buried

non assumpsit • he did not promise

non compos mentis • not of sound mind

non est factum • it is not his deed

non placet • not approved

nonagesiums • ninetieth

nonaginta • ninety

nonus • ninth

nota • female bastard

nota bene • note well

notarius • notary, secretary

nothus • male bastard

novem • nine

novembri • November

noverint universi per presentes me • know all men by these presents (Bond)

novus • new

nox • night

nulla bone • no goods

nulla poena sine lege • no punishment except by law

nullius filius • nobody's son, a bastard

numerus domus • house number

numerus serialis • serial number

nupt fuerant • were married

nupta • bride

nuptiae justae • legal marriage

nuptias • wedding, nuptials

nuptus • married

nurus • daughter-in-law

nutrix • wet-nurse

15

LATIN WORDS AND PHRASES
DEFINED - O

ob imminens mortis periculum • due to imminent danger of death, emergency baptism

obdormitus est • he fell asleep, died

obedientia • homage

obedio • obey

obiit • died

obiit eodem anno • died in the same year

obiit est • he died

obiit in coelibatu • died a bachelor

obiit infans • died in infancy

obiit infans septem • died a minor

obiit innotus • died a spinster

obiit juvenis • died in childhood

obiit sine prole • died without issue

obiit sine prole mascula • died without male issue

obitus • death

oblegantia • bond

obligatio civilis • civil obligation, legal obligation

observanda • observations or notes

obstetrix • midwife

occidens • west

octavus • eighth

octo • eight

octobris • October

octogesimus • eightieth

octoginta • eighty

oculus • eye

oculus dexter • right eye

oculus sinister • left eye

officium • office, duty, position

olator • oilman

omne hora • every hour

omne in die • once a day

omne mane • every morning

omne nocte • every night

Omnia terras et tenementa, prata, pascua, et pasturas cum sepibus, fossis et fossatis et cum omnibus aliis proficuis et suis pertinentiis quod habeo in villa. ● All lands and tenements, meadows, grazing land, and pasture with their hedges, banks, and ditches, and with all profits and their appurtenances which I have in the village.

omnibus ● to, by all

omnibus Christi fidelibus ● to all faithful in Christ (Quitclaim)

operarius ● labourer, worker

opilio ● shephered

oppidanus ● town resident

oppidum ● town

opus citatum ● the work cited, previously cited

oriens ● east

originis ● birth, origin

oriundus ● originating from, born in

orphanus ● orphan

ortus ● beginning, birth

os ● mouth

16

LATIN WORDS AND PHRASES
DEFINED - P

pacatio ● payment

pagina ● page

pagus ● village, district, canton

palatinatus ● county

pannarius ● draper

par ● equal, like

paraphernalia ● married workman's property

parentes ● parents

parochia ● parish

parochianus ● parishioner

parachus ● parish priest

pars actrix ● plaintiff

pars defendens ● defendant

partus ● birth

parvus ● small, little

pastor ● shepherd

pater ● father

pateat universis per presentes ● be it known by these presents (Quitclaim)

patrina ● godmother

patrini ● sponsors, godparents

patrinus ● godfather

patrinus fuit ● godfather was

patruelia ● cousin

patruelis ● cousin

patruus ● father's brother, uncle

patruus magnus ● father's uncle

patruus maior ● father's great-uncle

patruus maximus ● father's great-great-uncle

pauper ● poor

pedagogus ● schoolmaster, teacher

pellicarius ● skinner

per capita ● poll tax

per curiam ● by the court

per mensem ● by the month

per quod ● whereby, by which

per stirpes ● by stock, by descent, when a child(ren) inherited a deceased parent's portion in a will (Estate file)

perdono ● grant

peregrina ● foreigner, traveler

peregrinus ● foreigner, traveler

peritus ● deceased, perished

peritus est ● he perished, died

persona extranea ● individual outside the family group

persona publica ● notary

petens ● plaintiff

pictor ● painter

pilula ● pill

piscator ● fisherman

piscenarius ● fisherman

pistor ● baker, miller

platea ● street

plegagium liberum ● free pledge

plevina ● pledge

plumbarius ● plumber

plutus ● baptised

pomarius ● fruiterer

ponso ● marry

possessor ● landowner

post ● after

post cibum ● after meals

post meridiem ● after noon

posthumus ● born after father's death

pottarius ● potter

praesntibus testibus ● their presence as witnesses

prefectus ● magistrate

presentibus ● present, in the presence of

primus ● first

pro rata ● in proportion

pro re nata ● as needed, as required

pro re nata tussis ● as needed for cough

pro salute animae ● for the good of the soul

pro se ● on one's own behalf

pro servicia inde debita ● for the service due

proavia ● great-grandmother

proavus ● great-grandfather

progener ● grandson-in-law

proles ● issue, child

pronepos ● great-grandson

proneptis ● great-granddaughter

pronurus ● granddaughter-in-law

pudicus ● pure, chaste

puella ● girl

puer ● boy

puerperium ● childbirth

puerulus natus die ● a little boy was born on

pulvis ● powder

purgatus ● baptised

puta ● reputed

17

LATIN WORDS AND PHRASES
DEFINED - Q

quadragesimus • fourtieth

quadraginta • forty

quadraginta et unam libras sterlingorum • forty-one pounds sterling

quaeque • each, every

quære • unproven but probable

quæstio • question, inquiry

quamdiu se bene gesserit • during good behaviour

quantum meruit • as much as he has earned

quantum satis • as much as is sufficient

quaque ante merdiem • every morning

quaque die • once a day

quaque hora • every hour

quaque hora somni • every night at bedtime

quarrerius • quarryman

quater in die • four times a day

quartus • fourth

quartus decimus • fourteenth

quarum • of which, of whom

quassillarius • pedlar

quattro consanguineo • fourth degree of consanguinity, e.g. third cousins

quattuor • four

quattuordecim • fourteen

qui tacet consentire videtur • he who is silent implies consent

quid pro quo • something for something

quietaclamantia • quitclaim

quiete • peacefully

quinctilis • July

quindecim • fifteen

quingentesimus • five hundredth

guingenti • five hundred

quinquagesimus • fiftieth

quinquaginta • fifty

quinque • five

quintus • fifth

quintus decimus • fifteenth

quoad bona ● deceased a resident outside jurisdiction of the court

quoad omnia parish ● for all purposes

quoad sacra ● for sacred purposes

quod ego ● that I

quod vide ● which see

18

LATIN WORDS AND PHRASES
DEFINED - R

re infecta ● the matter unfinished, unproved will (Probate)

recipio ● recover

recognito ● inquest by jury

recognoso ● recognise

recompenso ● reward

rectum ● justice

reddendo ● by giving, duty or service

regeneratus est ● he was baptised

Regina ● Queen, noblewoman

Regis ● King

regnum ● kingdom

relicta ● widow

relictus ● widower, survivor

religio ● religion

remisisse, relaxasse et omni pro me et heredibus meis quietcla-
masse ● to have remitted, released, and entirely quitclaimed for
me and my heirs (Quitclaim)

renatus est ● he was baptised/baptized

requiescat in pace ● rest in peace, may she or he rest in peace

res ● thing, matter, issue

res furtivae ● stolen goods

rex ● king

ritus ● rite, ceremony

rogare ● beseech, implore

romanus ● Roman

rotarius ● wheelwright

rusticus ● peasant, farmer, rustic

19

LATIN WORDS AND PHRASES
DEFINED - S

Sacellanus • Chaplain

sacer • sacred

sacerdos • priest

Sacramentum Sanctus • Holy Sacrament

saeculum • century, generation

salus • health, welfare

sanctus • male saint

saponarius • soap maker

sartor • tailor

scabinus • judge

sciant presentes et futuri • know all men present and to come, let those present and future know (Deed, Quitclaim, Conveyance)

scorta • unmarried mother

Scotia • Scotland

scriptum • writing, document

se • oneself

secede • to separate, to withdraw

secundus • second

sede vacants • a will probated elsewhere during a vacancy in the normal court (Probate)

sedecim • sixteen

senilis • weak and old

sepelire • to bury

sepelivi • I buried

septem • seven

septem dies • week

septembris • September

septemdeim • seventeen

septentriones • north

septimana • week

Septimana Penosa • Holy Week

septimus • seventh

septimus decimus • seventeenth

septuaginta • seventy

sepult • buried

sepultorum liber • burial register

sepultum est • buried in

sepultura • burial

sepultus • buried

sepultus est • he was buried

sequens • the following

servus • servant, slave

sex • six

sexagesimus • sixtieth

sexaginata • sixty

sextilis • August

sextus • sixth

sextus decimus • sixteenth

sexus • sex

si • if

si opus sit • if the need arises, if necessary

sic • thus, so. In brackets—[*sic*]—immediately after a word: it says this even though I know it is an error

signetur • let it be labeled

signum • sign, mark, seal

simila • fine flour

singulus • to each

sobrinus • cousin

socer • father-in-law

socius • comrade, ally

socus • mother-in-law

solemanicatio • solemization, marriage

solidus • shilling

somnus • sleep

soror • sister

sororis filia • sister's daughter, niece

sororis filius • sister's son, nephew

speciarius • grocer

spirituales parentes • godparents

sponsa • bride, betrothed

sponsalia • marriage banns

sponsatus • married

sponsor • godparent

sponsoribus • sponsors, godparents

sponsus • groom, betrothed

spurius • illegitimate

stabularius • ostler

statim • immediately

Status Animarum • Status of Souls

status de manerio • state of the manor (legal standing of a manor)

status quo • maintain current position

stuprata • unmarried, with child

stuprator ● illigetimate child's

sub conditione ● under condition

sub nominae ● under the name

sub voce ● under the title

subsignatus ● signed, marked below

supradictus ● stated above

susceptores ● godparents

sutor ● shoemaker

syrupus ● syrup

20

LATIN WORDS AND PHRASES
DEFINED - T

tabella ● tablet

tabula ● list

tanquam ab intestao ● as of an intestate

tastator ● ale-taster

te ● you

telarius ● weaver

teleonarius ● tax collector

tempus ● time, date

ter in die ● three times a day

terra sacra ● cemetery

tertius ● third

tertio consanguineo ● third degree of consanguinity, e.g. second cousins

tertius decimus ● thirteenth

testes • witnesses

testamentum • will, testament

testibus • testors, witnesses

testis • witness

thorus • status

tinctura • tincture

tomus • volume

tonellarius • cooper

tonsor • barber

totum ius et clameu quod habui vel habere potui • all rights and claims I had or might have

totus • whole

transitus est • he died

tredecim • thirteen

tres • three

tricesimus • thirtieth

trigemini • triplets, triple

triginta • thirty

tritavia • great-great-great-great-grandmother

tritavus • great-great-great-great-grandfather

triturator • thresher

tumulatus • buried

21

LATIN WORDS AND PHRASES DEFINED - U

ultimo • last, latest

ultimus • last

ultimus haeres • last heir

unctio extrema • last rites

undecim • eleven

undecimus • eleventh

undevicesimus • nineteenth

undeviginti • nineteen

unguentum • ointment

unigenitus • only born

unus • one

urbs • city, town

ut dictum • as directed

uti possedetis • to possess [ownership of property]

uxor • wife

uxoratis • married

uxoris frater • [wife's] brother-in-law

uxoris soror • [wife's] sister-in-law

uxoro • marry

22

LATIN WORDS AND PHRASES DEFINED - V

vaccarius • cowherd

velle • will, testament

verborum obligatio • verbal obligation, obtained by question and answer

verbum • word

vesper • evening, west

vespere • evening

vestiarius • tailor

via • way, street, road

vicarius • substitute

Vicarius • Vicar

vicesimus • twentieth

vicesimus primus • twenty-first

vicesimus secundus • twenty-second

vicesimus tertis • twenty-third

vicesimus quartus • twenty-fourth

vicesimus quintus • twenty-fifth

vicesimus sextus • twenty-sixth

vicesimus septimus • twenty-seventh

vicesimus octavus • twenty-eighth

vicesimus nonus • twenty-ninth

vicinus • nearby, neighbouring/neighboring

vicus • village

vide • see

vide infra • see below

vide sub • see under

vide supra • see above

videlicet • namely, that is to say

vidua • widow

viduus • widower

viginti • twenty

viginti unus • twenty-one

viginti duo • twenty-two

viginti tres • twenty-three

viginti quattuor • twenty-four

viginti quinque • twenty-five

viginti sex • twenty-six

viginti septem • twenty-seven

viginti octo • twenty-eight

viginti novem • twenty-nine

villa • village, town

vinculo matrimonii • "of the marriage bond", complete dissolution of marriage

vinum • wine

vir • man

virgo • maiden, bride

vitam cessit • he parted, died

vitellarius • victualler

vitriarius • glazier

viventem • then living

volenti non fit injuria • if a person consents, the act cannot be injurous

vos • you

LATIN WORDS AND PHRASES
DEFINED - W

Currently there are no "W" words or phrases. Use this space to write any you discover.

LATIN WORDS AND PHRASES
DEFINED - X

Currently there are no "X" words. Use this space to write any you discover.

LATIN WORDS AND PHRASES
DEFINED - Y

Currently there are no "Y" words or phrases. Use this space to write any you discover.

LATIN WORDS AND PHRASES
DEFINED - Z

Currently there are no "Z" words or phrases. Use this space to write any you discover.

LATIN ABBREVIATIONS USED FOR
MONTHS OF THE YEAR

7^{ber} • September

8^{ber} • October

9^{ber} • November

10^{ber} • December

IX^{ber} • November

VII^{ber} • September

VIII^{ber} • October

X^{ber} • December

Take note there were not always twelve months in the year historically. Be aware of OS/NS, *old style* versus *new style,* as the Julian calendar enacted by Julius Caesar started in 46 A.D then changed to the Gregorian calendar starting in 1582 through 1923. The range of years covers when various countries across Europe accepted the calendar change. Though not an exhaustive list, Spain began using the Gregorian calendar in 1582 while Scotland did not adopt it until 1600. Falling far behind, England and its holdings did not adopt until 1752. Finally, Greece applied the new calendar in 1923!

LATIN ABBREVIATIONS FOR TERMS AND PHRASES - A

a.c. • *ante cibum* = before meals

A.D. • *Anno Domini* = In the year of our Lord

A.M. • *ante meridiem* = before midday, morning

Ad.n.b.c.-T. • *Admon (de) bonis non administratis cum-Testamentum* or *Admon* = of goods unadministered with will annexed

aeq. • *aequus* = equal

aq. • *aqua* = water

AUC • *anno urbis conditae* = the year of the founded city

LATIN ABBREVIATIONS FOR TERMS AND PHRASES - B

b.i.d. ● *bis in die* = twice a day

LATIN ABBREVIATIONS FOR TERMS
AND PHRASES - C

c. • *circa* = around, approximate

c. • *cum* = with

c.c. • *cum cibo* = with food

c.t.a. • *cum testamento annexo* = with will annexed

cf. • *confer* = compare with

conj. • *conjux* = wife

cop. • *copulation* = marriage

cret. • *creta* = chalk

31

LATIN ABBREVIATIONS FOR TERMS
AND PHRASES - D

d.b.n. • *de bonis non administratis* = of goods unadministered by

d.s.p. • *decessit sine prole* = died without issue surviving

d.s.p.f. • *decessit sine prole femina* = died without female issue

d.s.p.leg. • *decessit sine prole legitima* = died without legitimate issue

d.s.p.m. • *decessit sine prole mascula* = died without male issue

d.s.p.s. • *decessit sine prole superstes* = died without surviving issue

d.v.m. • *decessit vita matris* = died in mother's lifetime

d.v.p. • *decessit vita patris* = died in father's lifetime

de bo. non • *de bonis non administratis* = of goods unadminis-tered by

Dom. • *Dominica* = Sunday

LATIN ABBREVIATIONS FOR TERMS AND PHRASES - E

e.g. • *exempli gratia* = for example

et al. • et alii = and others

et ux • *et uxor* = and wife

etc. • *et cetera* = and so forth

ex. aq. • *ex aqua* = with water

LATIN ABBREVIATIONS FOR TERMS AND PHRASES - F

fil. leg. • *filius / filia legitimus* = a legitimate son / daughter of

fort. • *fortis* = strong

ft. mist. • *fortis mistura* = strong mixture

ft. cap • *fiat capsula* = make capsule

ft. ung. • *fiat unguentum* = make an ointment

LATIN ABBREVIATIONS FOR TERMS
AND PHRASES - G

Though there are no "G" abbreviations, use this space to note any you discover.

LATIN ABBREVIATIONS FOR TERMS AND PHRASES - H

hab. ● *habeo* = to have, to hold

h.s. ● *hora somni* = at bedtime

hyd. ● *hydragyrum* = Mercury

LATIN ABBREVIATIONS FOR TERMS AND PHRASES - I

i.c. • *inter cibos* = between meals

i.e. • *id est* = that is

i.m. • *intramuscular* = into the muscle

i.u. • *iure ux(oris)* = inherited by the right of his wife

ibid • *ibidem* = same place, book, date, etc.

inst. • *instante* = immediate, at the present moment

LATIN ABBREVIATIONS FOR TERMS AND PHRASES - J

Jur. • *Juratus* = sworn

LATIN ABBREVIATIONS FOR TERMS AND PHRASES - K

Though there are no "K" terms and phrases, use this space to note any you discover.

LATIN ABBREVIATIONS FOR TERMS AND PHRASES - L

l.p.r.p. • *legitimatus per rescriptum principis* = legitimate by subsequent marriage

l.s. • *locus sigilli* = the place of the seal [after a signature on a will]

LATIN ABBREVIATIONS FOR TERMS
AND PHRASES - M

mist. ● *mistura* = mixture

LATIN ABBREVIATIONS FOR TERMS AND PHRASES - N

n. • *natus* = born

N.B. • *nota bene* = note well

na. • *natus* = born

nat. • *natus* = born

LATIN ABBREVIATIONS FOR TERMS AND PHRASES - O

o.c. • *oculus sinister* = left eye

o.d. • *oculus dexter* = right eye

o.d. • *omne in die* = once a day

o.h. • *omne hora* = every hour

o.m. • *omne mane* = every morning

o.n. • *omne nocte* = every night

o.s.p.m. • *obiit sine prole mascula* = died without male issue

o.u. • *oculus uterque* = each eye

ob. • *obiit* = died

ob. coel. • *obiit in coelibatu* = died a bachelor

ob. inf. • *obiit infans* = died in infancy

ob. inf. set. • *obiit infans septem* = died a minor

ob. inn. • *obiit innotus* = died a spinster

ob. juv. • *obiit juvenis* = died in childhood

op. cit. • *opus citatum* = the work cited, previously cited

43

LATIN ABBREVIATIONS FOR TERMS
AND PHRASES - P

p.c. • *post cibum* = after meals

p.r.n. • *pro re nata* = as needed, as required

p.r.n. tuss. • *pro re nata tussis* = as needed for cough

pil. • *pilula* = pill

pts. • *in partibus transmarinis* = foreign parts, i.e., outside England, Ireland, Scotland, and Wales

pulv. • *pulvis* = powder

LATIN ABBREVIATIONS FOR TERMS
AND PHRASES - Q

q.a.m. • *quaque ante merdiem* = every morning

q.d. • *quaque die* = once a day

q.h. • *quaque hora* = every hour

q.h.s. • *quaque hora somni* = every night at bedtime

q.i.d. • *quater in die* = four times a day

q.s. • *quantum satis* = as much as is sufficient

q.v. • *quod vide* = which see

LATIN ABBREVIATIONS FOR TERMS AND PHRASES - R

R.I.P. • *requiescat in pace* = may she or he rest in peace

LATIN ABBREVIATIONS FOR TERMS
AND PHRASES - S

s.o.s. ● *si opus sit* = if the need arises, if necessary

sep. ● *sepultus* = buried

sepult ● *sepultus* = buried

sig. ● *signetur* = let it be labeled

sp. ● *sponsoribus* = sponsors, godparents

spur. ● *spurius* = illegitimate

stat. ● *statim* = immediately

syr. ● *syrupus* = syrup

LATIN ABBREVIATIONS FOR TERMS AND PHRASES - T

t.a.i. ● *tanquam ab intestao* = as of an intestate

t.i.d. ● *ter in die* = three times a day

tab. ● *tabella* = tablet

test. ● *testibus* = testor, witness

tinct. ● *tinctura* = tincture

LATIN ABBREVIATIONS FOR TERMS AND PHRASES - U

u. d. ● *ut dictum* = as directed

ult. ● *ultimo* = last

ung. ● *unguentum* = ointment

ut. dict. ● *ut dictum* = as directed

ux. ● *uxor* = wife

LATIN ABBREVIATIONS FOR TERMS AND PHRASES - V

v. infra • *vide infra* = see below

v. sub • *vide sub* = see under

v. supra • *vide supra* = see above

V.D.M. • *Verbi Dei Minister* = Minister of the Word of God

vid. • *vidua* = widow(er)

vin. • *vinum* = wine

viv. • *viventem* = then living

viz. • *videlicet* = namely

LATIN ABBREVIATIONS FOR TERMS AND PHRASES - W

Though there are no "W" abbreviations for terms and phrases, use this space to write any you discover.

LATIN ABBREVIATIONS FOR TERMS AND PHRASES - X

Though there are no "X" abbreviations for terms and phrases, use this space to write any you discover.

LATIN ABBREVIATIONS FOR TERMS
AND PHRASES - Y

Though there are no "Y" abbreviations for terms and phrases, use this space to write any you discover.

LATIN ABBREVIATIONS FOR TERMS AND PHRASES - Z

Though there are no "Z" abbreviations for terms and phrases, use this space to write any you discover.

MALE LATIN NAMES - A

Adamus • Adam

Adolfus • Adolf

Aegidius • Giles

Aemilius • Emile

Alanus • Alan

Alberedus • Alfred

Albertus • Albert

Alfonsus • Alphonse

Alfredus • Alfred

Aloisius • Aloysius

Andreas • Andrew

Anthonius • Anthony

Archibaldus • Archibald

Arcturus • Arthur

Arnoldus • Arnold

Arturus • Arthur

MALE LATIN NAMES - B

Barnabas • Barnabas, Barnaby

Bartholomaeus • Bartholomew

Basilius • Basil

Benedictus • Benedict

Benjaminus • Benjamin

Bernardus • Bernard

Bertoldus • Berthold

Bertrandus • Bertrand

Bonifatius • Boniface

Brianus • Brian

MALE LATIN NAMES - C

Carolus • Charles

Christianus • Christian

Christophorus • Christopher

Clarentius • Clarence

Clemens • Clement

Colandus • Colin

Conradus • Conrad

Constantinus • Constantine

Cornelius • Cornelius

Cuthbertus • Cuthbert

MALE LATIN NAMES - D

Danielus • Daniel

Davidus • David

Demetrius • Jeremiah

Dionysius • Dennis

Doninicus • Dominic

Dunechanus • Duncan

Duvenaldus • Donald

MALE LATIN NAMES - E

Eberardus ● Everard

Edmundus ● Edmund

Eduardus ● Edward

Egidius ● Giles

Elfredus ● Alfred

Ernestus ● Ernest

Erniscus ● Ernest

Eugenius ● Eugene

Eustachius ● Eustache

MALE LATIN NAMES - F

Fabianus • Fabian

Ferdinandus • Ferdinand

Francicus • Francis

Fridericus • Frederick

Fulcus • Fulk

MALE LATIN NAMES - G

Galferus • Walter

Galfridus • Geoffrey

Georgius • George

Geraldus • Gerald

Gerardus • Gerard

Gervasius • Gervase

Gilbertus • Gilbert

Godefridus • Godfrey

Godehardus • Goddard

Grahamus • Graham

Gregorius • Gregory

Gualcherius • Walter

Gualterus • Walter

Guido • Guy

Guilielmus • William

Gustavus • Gustave

MALE LATIN NAMES - H

Hamo ● Hamon

Haraldus ● Harold

Henricus ● Henry, Harry

Herbertus ● Herbert

Hermannus ● Herman

Hieremias ● Jeremiah

Hildebrandus ● Hildebrand

Horatius ● Horace

Hubertus ● Herbert

Hugo ● Hugh

Humfredus ● Humphrey

MALE LATIN NAMES - I

Ioachimus • Joachim

Isaacus • Isaac

Isaias • Isaiah

Ivo • Yves

Isidorus • Isidore

MALE LATIN NAMES - J

Jacobus • Jacob, James

Johannes • John

Johannulus • Johnny

Jordanus • Jordan

Josephus • Joseph

Justinus • Justin

MALE LATIN NAMES - K

Though there are no "K" male names included, write any you discover.

MALE LATIN NAMES - L

Laurentius • Lawrence

Leonardus • Leonard

Leonillus • Lionel

Leopoldus • Leopold

Levelinua • Llewellyn

Lorentius • Lawrence

Lotharius • Lothar

Lucas • Luke

Ludovicus • Louis, Lewis

MALE LATIN NAMES - M

Malachias • Malachi

Marcus • Mark

Martinus • Martin

Matthaeus • Matthew

Maximilianus • Maximilian

Meuricius • Maurice

Michaelis • Michael

Milo • Miles

Morganus • Morgan

Moyses • Moses

MALE LATIN NAMES - N

Natalis • Noel

Nicholaus • Nicholas

Nigellus • Nigel

Norbertus • Norbert

MALE LATIN NAMES - O

Olivarius ● Oliver

Omfreidus ● Humphrey

Osvaldus ● Oswald

MALE LATIN NAMES - P

Paschalis • Pascal

Patricius • Patrick

Paulus • Paul

Peregrinus • Peregrine

Petrus • Peter

Phillipus • Phillip

MALE LATIN NAMES - Q

Quintinus • Quentin

MALE LATIN NAMES - R

Radulfus • Ralph

Raimundus • Raymond

Rainerius • Rainier

Randolphus • Randolph

Radulphus • Ralph

Resus • Rhys

Ricardus • Richard

Richardus • Richard

Robertus • Robert

Rodericus • Roderick

Rodulfus • Rudolph

Rogerius • Roger

Rohelendus • Roland

Rolandus ● Roland

Romanus ● Romain

Ruertus ● Rupert

MALE LATIN NAMES - S

Sebastianus • Sebastian

Sigefridus • Siegfried

Sigismundus • Sigmund

Silvanus • Silas

Stephanus • Stephan, Stephen

MALE LATIN NAMES - T

Tedbaldus • Theobald

Tertius • (Though the word means "third", it was a given name for males possibly the third son.)

Thaddaeus • Thaddeus

Theoaldus • Theobald

Theodoricus • Theodric, Theodrick

Theodorus • Theodore

Timotheus • Timothy

Titus • Titus

MALE LATIN NAMES - U

Remember that the letters "U" and "V" often crossed in Latin usage.

Udalricus • Ulrich

Umfridus • Humphrey

Urbanus • Urban

MALE LATIN NAMES - V

Remember the Latin letters "U" and "V" often crossed in Latin usage.

Valdemarus • Waldemar

Valentinus • Valentine

Valerianus • Valerian

Venceslaus • Wenceslas

Vergilius • Virgil

Vido • Guy

Vilfridus • Wilfred

Villefridus • Wilfred

Vincentius • Vincent

MALE LATIN NAMES - W

Though the letter "W" isn't in the Latin alphabet, these names may appear in historical research as a Latin version.

Walterus • Walter

Wilhelmus • William

Willelmus • William

MALE LATIN NAMES - X

Xtianus • Christian

Xoforus • Christopher

Xtopherus • Christopher

MALE LATIN NAMES - Y

Yvonus ● Yves, Ives

MALE LATIN NAMES - Z

Though there are no "Z" male names, use this space to write any you discover.

FEMALE LATIN NAMES - A

Adelaidis • Adelaide

Aemilia • Emily

Agneta • Agnes

Alexia • Alice

Alianora • Eleanor

Alicia • Alice

Alitia • Alice

Aloisia • Louise

Amabilla • Mabel

Amia • Amy

Anabilia • Annabel

Anicia • Annis

Anna • Anna, Ann

Aurelia • Aurora

FEMALE LATIN NAMES - B

Beatrix ● Beatrice

Berta ● Bertha

Blanca ● Blanche

Brigida ● Bridget

Brigitta ● Bridget

FEMALE LATIN NAMES - C

Caecilia • Cecilia

Caius • Kay

Camillia • Camille

Carola • Carol

Catalina • Catherine

Catherina • Catherine, Katherine

Clelia • Chloe

Clemintina • Clementine

Coelia • Celia

Constantia • Constance

Christina • Christine

FEMALE LATIN NAMES - D

Dacia • (No Anglicized version)

Dana • Dana (God is my Judge)

Dayna • Dayna (Feminine form of Daniel)

Debelia • Bridget

Delicia • (Feminine form of Delicious, meaning: Pleasant)

Diana/Digna/Digne • Diana/Diann(a)/Diahan/Diane/Dina

Didoh • Queen

Dionisia • Denise

Dorothea • Dorothy

Drusilla • (No Anglicized form, meaning: Dew)

FEMALE LATIN NAMES - E

Eleanora ● Eleanor

Elinora ● Eleanor

Elisabetha ● Elisabeth

Elizabeta ● Elizabeth

Emelina ● Emily

Ermina ● Hermine

Ethelreda ● Audrey

Eva ● Eve

FEMALE LATIN NAMES - F

Felicia ● Phyllis

Felicitas ● Felicity

Fida ● Faith

Fides ● Faith

Francisca ● Frances

FEMALE LATIN NAMES - G

Gabriela • Gabriella

Gertrudis • Gertrude

Gratia • Grace

Guinevra • Winifred

FEMALE LATIN NAMES - H

Hadriana • Adrian

Helena • Helen, Ellen, Eleanor

Henrica • Henriette

Hildegardis • Hildegarde

Honoria • Honor

FEMALE LATIN NAMES - I

Imania ● Emma

Isabella ● Isabel

FEMALE LATIN NAMES - J

Jodoca • Joyce

Johanna • Joan, Jane

Joscia • Joyce

Josepha • Josephine

Juditha • Judith

Julia • Julie, Julia

Juliana • Gillian

FEMALE LATIN NAMES - K

Because the letter "K" is not in the Latin alphabet, you're not likely to find any, but these names are included as they may be historically used in more modern documents. Use this space to write what you discover.

Kliara ● Clara

Kamella ● Camilla/Camellia

FEMALE LATIN NAMES - L

Laetitia ● Letitia, Lettice

Letje ● Letha/Lettie

Lucia ● Lucy

FEMALE LATIN NAMES - M

Mabilla ● Mabel

Magdalena ● Madeleine

Margareta ● Margaret

Margeria ● Margery

Maria ● Mary, Maria, Marie

Maria Anna ● Marianne

Marianna ● Mary Ann, Marion

Marta ● Martha

Matilda ● Maud

Mathildis ● Mathilda

Matildis ● Mathilda

Mercia ● Mercy

Misericordia ● Mercy

FEMALE LATIN NAMES - N

Nicolaa ● Nicola

Nebulia ● Misty

FEMALE LATIN NAMES - O

Odilia ● Odile

Omoria/Onoria ● Honor

Orseline ● Ursula

FEMALE LATIN NAMES - P

Paulina ● Pauline

Petara ● Petra (feminine form of Peter)

Phillida ● Phyllis

Piencia ● Bianca/Biance

Prudentia ● Prudence

FEMALE LATIN NAMES - Q

Quinn • Quinn (Descendant of Cuinn; Fifth born)

Quentin/Quinta • Queen (From the queen's land)

Quintilia • May

FEMALE LATIN NAMES - R

Rosa • Rose

Rosalia • Rosalie

Rosalinda • Rosalind

Rosamunda • Rosamund

FEMALE LATIN NAMES - S

Seisillus • Cecil

Sibella • Sybil

Stephania • Stephany

FEMALE LATIN NAMES - T

Tacita • *(meaning: to be silent, no known Anglicized name)*

Tefia • Tiffy/Taffie

Teresia • Teresa

Thekla • (meaning: God's Flame, no known Anglicized name)

FEMALE LATIN NAMES - U

Remember the Latin letters "U" and "V" sometimes cross in Latin words and names.

Ulma ● Alma

FEMALE LATIN NAMES - V

Remember the Latin letters "U" and "V" sometimes cross in Latin words and names.

Viola • Violet

Visia • (*strength/vigor, no Anglicized version*)

Vitel • Fidela

FEMALE LATIN NAMES - W

Though "W" isn't in the Latin alphabet, you may run into historical latin-based names. Use this space to add more. Here's a few you could see in historical documents.

Wavia ● (meaning: foreign woman) A similar name is Ava.

Wera/Jera ● Vera

FEMALE LATIN NAMES - X

Though there are not many "X" female names, write any you discover.

FEMALE LATIN NAMES - Y

Though there are not often Latin "Y" female names, write any you discover.

FEMALE LATIN NAMES - Z

Though there are no "Z" Latin female names, write any Latin-based names you discover here.

GENEALOGY COURSES

International Institute of Genealogical Studies courses these materials compliment include:

Latin for Genealogists

Palaeography: Reading and Understanding Historical Documents

Skills: Transcribing, Abstracting and Extracting

American: Cemetery Records

American: Court Records

American: Land Records

American: Probate Records

American: Religious Records-Part 1

American: Religious Records-Part 2

Canadian: Land Records-Part 1

Canadian: Land Records-Part 2

248

Scottish: Wills and Testaments

Research: Dutch Ancestors in the Netherlands

Research: U.S. Colonial New England Ancestors

To learn more about these online courses, visit **Genealogical-Studies.com**.

BIBLIOGRAPHY

In addition to course content online at the International Institute of Genealogical Studies, found at GenealogicalStudies.com, these books were helpful to our staff as we developed this reference tool for you:

Jensen, C. Russell, *Parish Register Latin: An Introduction* (Vita Nova Books, 1989).

Shea, Jonathan D., and William F. Hoffman, *Following the Paper Trail: A Multilingual Translation Guide* (Teaneck, New Jersey: Avotaynu, 1994).

NOTES:

www.ingramcontent.com/pod-product-compliance
Lightning Source LLC
Chambersburg PA
CBHW062131040426
42335CB00039B/1966